Classic Recipes of
PORTUGAL

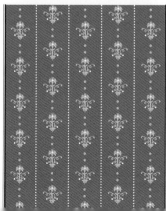

Classic Recipes of
PORTUGAL

TRADITIONAL FOOD AND COOKING
IN 25 AUTHENTIC DISHES

MIGUEL DE CASTRO E SILVA

LORENZ BOOKS

This edition is published by
Lorenz Books
an imprint of Anness Publishing Ltd
info@anness.com
www.lorenzbooks.com
www.annesspublishing.com

If you like the images in this book and
would like to investigate using them for
publishing, promotions or advertising,
please visit our website
www.practicalpictures.com for more
information.

Publisher: Joanna Lorenz
Editor: Helen Sudell
Designer: Nigel Partridge
Recipe Photography: William Lingwood
Food Stylist: Lucy McKelvie
Prop Stylist: Helen Trent
Production Controller: Ben Worley

A CIP catalogue record for this book is
available from the British Library

PUBLISHER'S NOTE

Although the advice and information in this
book are believed to be accurate and true
at the time of going to press, neither the
author nor the publisher can accept any
legal responsibility or liability for any errors
or omissions that may have been made nor
for any inaccuracies nor for any loss, harm
or injury that comes about from following
instructions or advice in this book.

PUBLISHER'S ACKNOWLEDGMENTS

The Publisher would like to thank the
following agencies for the use of their
images. Istock p 6, p8, p 9 (both).
Alamy p10 (both), p11

Previously published as part of a larger
volume The Food and Cooking of Portugal.

COOK'S NOTES

Bracketed terms are intended for American
readers. For all recipes, quantities are given
in both metric and imperial measures and,
where appropriate, in standard cups and
spoons. Follow one set of measures, but
not a mixture, because they are not
interchangeable.

Standard spoon and cup measures are
level. 1 tsp = 5ml, 1 tbsp = 15ml, 1 cup =
250ml/8fl oz. Australian standard
tablespoons are 20ml. Australian readers
should use 3 tsp in place of 1 tbsp for
measuring small quantities.

American pints are 16fl oz/2 cups.
American readers should use 20fl oz/2.5
cups in place of 1 pint when measuring
liquids.

Electric oven temperatures in this book are
for conventional ovens. When using a fan
oven, the temperature will probably need to
be reduced by about 10–20°C/20–40°F.
Since ovens vary, you should check with
your manufacturer's instruction book for
guidance.

The nutritional analysis given for each
recipe is calculated per portion (i.e. serving
or item), unless otherwise stated. If the
recipe gives a range, such as Serves 4–6,
then the nutritional analysis will be for the
smaller portion size, i.e. 6 servings. The
analysis does not include optional
ingredients, such as salt added to taste.

Medium (US large) eggs are used unless
otherwise stated.

Contents

Introduction

Portugal is a land of amazing variety. From the remote and mountainous region in the north to the sun-kissed beaches of the Algarve in the south, and from the historic borders with Spain in the east to the wild Atlantic Ocean in the west, this small country accommodates many different kinds of climate, culture and cuisine. Traditional fare has always been based around wholesome, robust meals for farmers and fishermen using fresh, local ingredients, and this emphasis still strongly informs the contemporary diet.

Left: The brightly coloured houses and red roof tiles of the Alfama district of Lisbon.

Portuguese Cuisine

Many Portuguese people consider food and drink to be one of the most important parts of their life. Breakfast is a quick affair of coffee and rolls. Lunch takes longer, and often consists of one main course – in a restaurant, the *prato do dia* (dish of the day) is very popular with locals. The serious eating of the day is in the evening, and Sunday lunch with the extended family is a big occasion, which you skip at your peril.

One delightful food tradition enjoyed by the Portuguese and their visitors in bars, cafés and

Below: Egg pastries and coffee are traditional breakfast fare.

Above: Petiscos, such as these figs wrapped in pancetta, are served with drinks.

restaurants is *petiscos*. These are delicious morsels of meat, fish or vegetables with bread and a glass or two of wine.

Exotic discoveries

Over the centuries, Portugal has had the good fortune to discover and grow many fine ingredients for cooking. Exotic spices, nuts, coffee and chilli peppers came from trading routes opening up to India, Africa and Brazil. It is these new flavours, combined with the natural abundance of fresh fish, seafood, locally grown meat and

aromatic herbs from the hillsides, that makes Portuguese cuisine so rich and fresh.

Native favourites

Traditionally Portuguese cooks have had to be both frugal and resourceful in making full use of native animals for food, particularly the pig from which come sausages, *morcela* (a spicy black pudding), and cured ham as well as the main pork cuts. Other dishes are based on lamb, goat and poultry.

Around the coast, fish and seafood are the main ingredients. Many a Portuguese *caldeirada* (fish stew) is based on large amounts of vegetables with white wine and whatever fish is available. The cod caught by Portuguese fishermen far away in the cold waters of the North Atlantic used to be salted to preserve it. This has become such a favourite that *bacalhau* (salt cod) is known as 'the faithful friend'.

Right: Fish is hung out to dry during the summer months.

Food and Festivals

Portugal's rich cultural and religious heritage is reflected in the many festivals celebrated with great gusto throughout the year. Often, a festival's religious origins combine with a healthy attention to the food and drink associated with it.

New Year

The celebrations for New Year start with special church services and people eat twelve grapes as the church bells strike

Below: The streets of Ponta Delgada before the procession.

midnight, which guarantees a happy twelve months ahead.

At Epiphany (6 January), a family feast is often held with a special ring-shaped cake containing small gifts for the children and, somewhere hidden within it, one dried broad bean. The lucky finder of the bean becomes king for the day, but has to promise to make the cake next year.

February

Before the restrictions of Lent begin on Ash Wednesday, carnivals are held in many Portuguese cities. Parties and dances are common throughout the country, and it's a time of licence when people act irresponsibly. Battles with eggs, flour and water used to take place, but now the festivities are more likely to consist of parades and dressing up.

Easter

As a country with a strong religious tradition, there are many Easter festivals. Starting on Palm Sunday and continuing throughout Holy Week, there are church processions around villages and towns. A *Folar* cake is made to celebrate Easter, decorated with hard-boiled eggs on top of a sweet dough.

Whitsun

At Pentecost, special feasts are held, traditionally in aid of the poor. Tables covered with food are laid out in the street. The feasting can go on for eleven days until Corpus Christi. In Ponta Delgada on San Miguel, the procession passes over a long carpet of flower petals.

July

The *Festa Dos Tabuleiros* is held in the central city of Tomar every other year. A Thanksgiving festival for harvest time, food plays a major part alongside dancing, processions and other entertainments. Processions of girls wear flowers as well as small loaves of bread in their huge headdresses to symbolize the harvest. Bread, wine and meat are blessed by priests and then distributed to the poor.

September

A fisherman's festival is held in Nazare each September. This is in honour of Our Lady of Nazare, where a chapel was built by Dom Fuas, a grateful hunter who had a sudden vision of the Virgin, which stopped him from falling off a cliff in thick fog. The local fishermen adopted the chapel as a centre of pilgrimage and give thanks for Our Lady's protection against the perils of the sea.

Below: The chapel of Our Lady of Nazare.

November

The dead are remembered on 1 November, All Saints' Day. In the past, food was taken by family members into local churchyards to eat; nowadays open-air feasts are more likely to be held in the streets. The grown-ups drink wine and eat chestnuts, while the children prefer eating little sugar cakes flavoured with cinnamon and herbs that are specially made for this day.

The traditional day for slaughtering the family pig falls on 11 November, the festival of

Above: The huge headdresses at the Festa dos Tabuleiros.

Sao Martinho. The feasts include more Portuguese wine and roasted whole chestnuts – seasonal produce which goes very well with pork.

Christmas

The Portuguese love a family reunion, and this is a good excuse to eat and drink around a burning *cepo de natal* (Yule log). After the festivities, crumbs are left on the hearth or food on the table for wandering ghosts.

Classic Ingredients

The traditional Portuguese diet is very similar to that eaten in many Mediterranean countries. It is based on the simplest and tastiest of foods, such as bread, rice, olive oil, garlic, tomatoes and herbs. In addition to these basic elements, the Portuguese cook will add small amounts of meat and fish and a variety of spices to make a vibrant dish.

Meat

Pork, lamb and poultry figure largely in Portuguese recipes, but were originally a treat availably only to noblemen. The exception was around the time

Below: Morcela (blood sausage) is made from pig's blood.

of the slaughter of the family pig, where every single part was eaten, including the pig's stomach (tripe) and blood.

Poultry and lamb dishes are usually cooked slowly with tomatoes or other vegetables and herbs, and bulked out with either rice or potatoes. Beef is not a common dish in Portugal, but when it is eaten, it is usually in the form of a thin slice of steak quickly fried, which sometimes comes with an egg on top and is accompanied by potatoes and olives.

Fish and shellfish

Portugal has many great recipes for fish. All kinds of fish and shellfish are eaten – sardines, prawns (shrimp), sea bass, swordfish, octopus, tuna, crab, mackerel, clams, oysters – mainly freshly grilled (broiled) or baked in the oven with garlic, herbs and wine. There are a couple of exceptions to the rule of putting fish straight from the sea on to the plate, however. One is *caldeirada*, a stew of any available fish or shellfish, which

is simmered for a long time (and is often cooked at weekends in the busy 21st century).

The other exception is *bacalhau*, salted cod, a staple ingredient of Portuguese cooking. To preserve the fish, fishermen, hundreds of miles from home, used to clean and gut them on board the boat and kept adding layers of salt to the flattened cod until the hold was full. Only then would they turn for home, where the fish were dried in the sun.

Bacalhau has to be de-salted and hydrated before it can be cooked. It is divided into pieces and then soaked in several changes of fresh water over two days. Once most of the salt has been removed it is cooked and eaten straight away. You can buy de-salted *bacalhau* from supermarkets. Typical dishes combine the cod with potatoes, eggs, pancakes or bread for a substantial meal.

Right: Prawns are fished around the mainland coastline and the two large island regions.

Above: Olives and olive oil feature largely in the diet.

Olives and olive oil

These ingredients are universally used. Each region has its own varieties of olives. The northern regions' olive oil is light, fresh and a brilliant green in colour; in the central Beiras, there is a flavour of almonds and dried fruit; in the hot southern region the olive oil is more mature and blends particularly well with cooked food.

Olive oil is used both in frying and grilling fresh fish, and in marinating meat and fish for longer. It is also a major part of any salad dressing. Olives are typically marinated with olive oil, oregano and slices of lemon.

Dairy Produce

The dairy industry in Portugal is based around cheese and butter rather than cow's milk. Cheese is rarely used for cooking. It is more often eaten on its own as part of an evening meal.

The Portuguese make delicious creamy cheeses from goat's milk or sheep's milk. *Serra da Estrela* and *Serpa* cheese are favourites. These creamy, strongly flavoured cheeses can be eaten with a spoon, or cut into slices when more solid and mature.

Queijo fresco, a fresh, young cheese made with goat's milk, makes a light first course sprinkled with salt and accompanied by a tomato and oregano salad.

Vegetables

Many vegetables are grown in the accommodating climate but the most universal are tomatoes and potatoes. Both of these were brought from the New World in the 15th and 16th centuries and rapidly became

Above: The sweet Serpa cheese from the Alentejo.

the basis of all kinds of dishes, from salads to stews and soups to pies. Another essential ingredient is the fiery chilli peppers (piri piri) that were brought to Portugal from Brazil.

One of the most popular dishes in Portugal is *caldo verde*, the green cabbage soup made in the north. This is real solid peasant food, made with finely shredded *couve galega* (Galician cabbage), as well as a few chunks of sausage.

Vegetables add colour, flavour and nutritional value to many Portuguese dishes. The vivid green of broad (fava) beans, green beans, cabbage and asparagus is balanced in the stew by bright red tomatoes and (bell) peppers, and paler turnips, pumpkins, onions, garlic and potatoes.

Dried beans, peas and chestnuts

Legumes (beans and peas) have always been dried as a part of any peasant cuisine and many Portuguese stews consist of large amounts of dried beans or chickpeas with small amounts of meat or fish, for example the basic bean stew, *feijoada*. In the past, meat from the family pig could be braised slowly with chickpeas and wild mushrooms.

Below: Dried beans are served with pork, chicken and fish.

Or a hare would be combined with white haricot (navy) beans in a strong-tasting stew, *lebre com feijao*.

Wild chestnuts are used in savoury braised recipes, and are also eaten on their own in the autumn.

Bread and rice

In Portugal, the very many types of bread are not only a base for cheese, a mopper-up of juices or a light breakfast, bread is also added to soup to thicken it.

Rice features in many recipes, both savoury and sweet. You can find rice in soups, in stews of meat or fish, as the basis of a risotto-like *arroz de marisco* (seafood rice) or just with honey or sugar and topped with cinnamon in the Portuguese version of rice pudding, *arroz doce*.

Fruits, nuts and sweet things

Citrus fruits were brought to the country by the Moors in the 8th century, along with almonds and figs, and these all flourish in the

Above: Almonds feature in many Portuguese desserts.

hot summers and warm winters of the Algarve and the Douro region. Fruits and almonds are often combined with honey and sponge cake, eggs or pastry to make dessert.

There is a delightful tradition, from the 17th century, when the nuns in the Azores baked cakes and pastries to raise funds for their convent. The names given to these tasty morsels reveal quite a sense of humour among the sisters – *papos de anjo* (angels' cheeks) and *barrigas de freiras* (nuns' bellies), to name but two – and they are very sweet confections of flour, egg and sugar.

Portuguese Flavours

Portugal is so rich in locally sourced ingredients that it has given great inspiration to the inventive cook over the centuries, ever since the Romans first marched here and stopped at the Atlantic Ocean, thinking it was the edge of the world. From pork ribs to shellfish, from sardines to sheep's cheese, and from chestnuts to cabbage, Portuguese food is a riot of flavour and freshness, using everything this favourable climate can provide. This essential collection of recipes offer a lively introduction to an exciting cuisine.

Left: Fresh, locally sourced ingredients form the basis of Portuguese cooking.

Tomato Salad with Peppers and Oregano
Tomate com pimentos marinados e oregãos

Serves 4–6

2 marinated (bell) peppers, drained
6 ripe tomatoes, sliced
15ml/1 tbsp chopped fresh oregano
75ml/5 tbsp olive oil
30ml/2 tbsp white wine vinegar
sea salt

1 If the marinated peppers are in large pieces, cut them into strips. Arrange the tomato slices and pepper strips on a serving dish, sprinkle with the oregano and season to taste with sea salt.

2 Whisk together the olive oil and vinegar in a jug or pitcher and pour the dressing over the salad. Serve immediately or cover and chill in the refrigerator until required.

COOK'S TIP
To make the marinated peppers yourself wrap two peppers in foil and place on a baking sheet. Cook in a preheated oven at 180°C/350°F/Gas 4, or under a preheated grill (broiler), turning occasionally, for 20–30 minutes, until tender. Unwrap and when cool, peel the peppers, then halve and seed. Cut the flesh into strips and pack into a screw-top jar. Add olive oil to cover, close and store in the refrigerator for up to 6 days.

The Portuguese usually prepare this refreshing appetizer with home-grown tomatoes for maximum flavour and sweetness. They combine superbly with marinated peppers, which, because they have been well roasted before soaking, are sweeter and more digestible than raw ones.

Marinated Mushrooms
Cogumelos marinados

Serves 4

400g/14oz mixed mushrooms, such
  as chestnut and oyster
  mushrooms
30ml/2 tbsp olive oil
200g/7oz raw ham, sausages and
  bacon, diced
2 garlic cloves, finely chopped
15–30ml/1–2 tbsp white wine
  vinegar
45ml/3 tbsp chopped fresh parsley

This dish is usually served cold but tastes equally good hot from the pan. Use as many mushroom varieties as you like to make the most of their various flavours and textures. This is a useful way of using up a solitary sausage or a couple of slices of bacon or ham.

1 Wipe the mushrooms clean with a clean, damp cloth and cut or tear the larger ones in half or quarters.

2 Heat the olive oil in a frying pan. Add the meat and cook over a low heat, stirring frequently, for about 5 minutes.

3 Add the mushrooms, increase the heat to high and cook, stirring constantly, for 5 minutes. Add the garlic and 15ml/1 tbsp of the vinegar and cook for 1 minute more.

4 Remove the pan from the heat and stir in the parsley. Serve immediately or, if you want to serve the mushrooms cold, add the remaining vinegar and leave to cool.

VARIATION
When served hot, these mushrooms also go well with scrambled eggs.

Green Beans Tempura
Peixinhos da horta

Serves 4

400g/14oz green beans
100g/3¾oz/scant 1 cup plain
  (all-purpose) flour
1 egg
vegetable oil, for deep-frying
salt

1 Trim the beans and blanch them in a large pan of boiling water for 1 minute. Drain and refresh in iced water, then drain again well.

2 Sift the flour into a bowl and stir in enough cold water to make a medium paste. Add the egg and beat well, then season with salt.

3 Heat the oil in a large pan or deep-fryer to 170°C/340°F or until a cube of day-old bread browns in 40 seconds. Dip the beans in the batter to coat, add to the hot oil and deep-fry until crisp and golden brown. Drain on kitchen paper and serve immediately.

VARIATION
While not traditionally Portuguese, you can prepare other vegetables in the same way. Try mushrooms, red (bell) pepper strips or carrots cut into thin batons.

A literal translation of peixinhos da horta is "from the field where you plant vegetables". The dish is distinguished by the green beans, which are coated in a light tempura batter. This cooking technique is thought to have been taken to Japan by Portuguese sailors in the early days of exploration.

Sardines in Onion and Tomato Marinade
Sardinhas de escabeche

Serves 4–6

12 sardines, cleaned
plain (all-purpose) flour, for dusting
150ml/¼ pint/⅔ cup olive oil
2 onions, halved and thinly sliced
3 bay leaves
2 garlic cloves, chopped
150ml/¼ pint/⅔ cup white wine
    vinegar
2 ripe tomatoes, diced
sea salt
crusty bread, to serve

Both fish and poultry are frequently marinated in Portuguese cooking. The basic marinade consists of onion, garlic, bay leaves and good-quality wine vinegar, to which tomatoes or other vegetables may be added. The sardines that are fished off Portugal's cold Atlantic coast are particularly fine.

1 Dust the sardines with flour, shaking off any excess. Heat 75ml/5 tbsp of the olive oil in a heavy frying pan. Add the sardines, in batches, and cook over a medium heat, for about 1 minute each side. Remove with a slotted spatula and drain on kitchen paper.

2 In a clean pan, cook the onions, bay leaves and garlic with the rest of the olive oil over a low heat, stirring occasionally, for about 5 minutes, until softened. Add the vinegar and the tomatoes, and season with sea salt to taste.

3 Return the sardines to the pan. If they are not completely covered, add a little water or some more vinegar. Cook for a few minutes. Transfer the mixture to a deep plate, allow to cool and leave to marinate in the refrigerator for 3 days. Serve with crusty bread.

Clams with Fresh Coriander
Amêijoas à Bulhão Pato

Serves 4

600g/1lb 6oz live clams
100ml/3½fl oz/scant ½ cup olive oil
2 garlic cloves, very finely chopped
1 lemon
1 bunch of fresh coriander (cilantro),
  chopped

This is the most common way to prepare clams in Portugal and also one of the most effective ways to enjoy their flavour. The smaller black-shelled clams found along Portugal's Atlantic coast are ideal, but there are many excellent types to be found all over the world. For a more substantial main dish, add butter beans and mashed tomato and serve with crusty bread.

1 Scrub the clams under cold running water. Discard any with broken shells or that do not shut immediately when sharply tapped.

2 Heat the olive oil in a large, heavy pan. Add the clams and garlic, cover with a tight-fitting lid and cook, shaking the pan frequently, for 3–5 minutes, until the shells open. Discard any that remain closed.

3 Halve the lemon and then squeeze the juice from one half into a bowl. Cut the other lemon half into wedges. Add the coriander and lemon juice to the clams and serve immediately with the lemon wedges.

COOK'S TIP
All shellfish deteriorates very rapidly once out of the sea. Buy clams from a reputable supplier and cook them on the day of purchase. It is unwise to collect clams from the beach because of the risk of pollution.

Small Chicken Pies Empada de galinha

Makes about 12

1 chicken, weighing 1.6–2kg/
    3½–4½lb
45ml/3 tbsp olive oil
1 sausage, weighing about 250g/9oz
150g/5oz bacon
1 garlic clove
10 black peppercorns
1 onion stuck with 2 cloves
1 bunch of parsley, chopped
4 thyme or marjoram sprigs
juice of 1 lemon or 60ml/4 tbsp white
    wine vinegar
butter, for greasing
500g/1¼lb puff pastry, thawed if
    frozen
plain (all-purpose) flour, for dusting
2 egg yolks, lightly beaten
salt

1 Cut the chicken into pieces. Heat the oil in a large, heavy pan. Add the chicken pieces and cook over a medium-low heat, turning occasionally, for about 10 minutes, until golden brown on all sides.

2 Add the sausage, bacon, garlic, peppercorns, onion, parsley, thyme and lemon juice or vinegar. Pour in enough water to cover and bring to the boil. Lower the heat, cover and simmer for 1–1½ hours, until tender.

3 Remove all the meat from the stock with a slotted spoon. Return the stock to the heat and cook on a medium heat, uncovered, until slightly reduced. Strain the stock into a bowl and season with salt to taste.

4 Remove and discard the chicken skin and bones and cut the meat into small pieces. Cut the sausage and bacon into small pieces. Mix all the meat together. Preheat the oven to 200°C/400°F/Gas 6. Grease a 12-cup muffin tin or pan with butter.

5 Roll out the pastry thinly on a lightly floured surface and stamp out 12 rounds with a 7.5cm/3in cutter. Gather the trimmings together and roll out thinly again, then stamp out 12 rounds with a 6cm/2½in cutter.

6 Place the larger rounds in the cups of the prepared tin, pressing the pastry to the side, and divide the meat among them. Spoon in a little stock, then brush the edges with beaten egg yolk and cover with the smaller rounds, pinching the edges to seal. Brush the remaining egg yolk over the top and make a small hole in the centre of each pie.

7 Bake for 15–25 minutes, until golden brown. Remove from the oven and leave to cool before serving.

These little pies can be filled with different kinds of meat, although chicken is the most popular. They make a tempting afternoon snack or you could have two or three of them with a refreshing salad for a delicious light lunch.

Chestnut and White Bean Soup
Sopa de castanhas e feijão branco

Serves 4

100g/3¾oz/½ cup dried haricot
 beans, soaked overnight in cold
 water and drained
90g/3½oz peeled chestnuts, thawed
 if frozen
1 bay leaf
50ml/2fl oz/¼ cup olive oil
1 onion, chopped
salt

1 Put the beans, chestnuts and bay leaf in a pan, pour in 1 litre/1¾ pints/4 cups of water and bring to the boil. Lower the heat and cook for about 1½ hours, until tender.

2 Meanwhile, heat the oil in a frying pan. Add the onion and cook over a low heat, stirring occasionally, for 5 minutes, until softened. Add it to the soup. Season to taste with salt, remove and discard the bay leaf and mash the beans and chestnuts with a fork. Serve immediately.

COOK'S TIP
If using fresh chestnuts, do not store them for more than a week. The easiest way to shell them and remove their inner skins is to make a small cut in each one and par-boil or roast in the oven at 180°C/350°F/Gas 4 for about 5 minutes. Remove the shells and rub off the skins with a dish towel. Peeled frozen chestnuts are a simpler option.

VARIATION
You can also make this soup with fresh white beans in the summer.

In the northern Minho, this soup was once prepared during Lent. It is quite substantial and was a good way of supplying energy to the workers. Chestnuts have been produced on the peninsula for a long time – well before potatoes, which were only "recently" imported from the Americas. As a result, chestnuts feature in many dishes, especially in the north.

Green Bean and Cabbage Soup
Sopa de feijão verde com segurelha

Serves 4

500g/1¼lb floury potatoes, cut into
  pieces
2 onions, chopped
300g/11oz Savoy cabbage
300g/11oz green beans, cut into
  1cm/½in lengths
1 small bunch of fresh summer
  savory, chopped
50ml/2fl oz/¼ cup olive oil
salt

1 Put the potatoes and onions in a large pan, add 1 litre/1¾ pints/4 cups water and bring to the boil. Cover and simmer for about 20 minutes, until tender.

2 Transfer the potatoes and onions and cooking liquid to a blender or food processor and process to a purée. Return to the rinsed-out pan.

3 Cut the cabbage in quarters, cut out the core and slice in 2.5cm/1in pieces. Add the cabbage, the beans and summer savory to the pan and cook over a medium heat for a few minutes, until the cabbage is cooked, and the beans are tender but still slightly crisp.

4 Season with salt to taste, stir in the olive oil and serve immediately.

This soup is found all over Portugal, but it is most popular in the central Ribatejo region. Here, the locals consider the addition of summer savory as essential to the recipe's success, and this aromatic, pungent herb does have a natural affinity with all kinds of beans.

Tomato Soup
Tomatada

Serves 4

50ml/2fl oz/¼ cup olive oil

1 onion, chopped

1 small sausage, preferably from
    black pork, cut into small pieces

1 garlic clove, chopped

4 ripe tomatoes, peeled, seeded and
    diced

1 fresh oregano sprig

1 litre/1¾ pints/4 cups chicken stock
    or water

4 small slices of dry bread, cut into
    cubes

15ml/1 tbsp chopped fresh coriander
    (cilantro)

salt

*The bread makes this both
a nourishing and substantial
soup. The recipe originates
in Alentejo, in southern
Portugal, where poor people
created fantastic soups
simply with water and a
combination of wild herbs
and vegetables, olive oil
and, always, bread.*

1 Heat the oil in a large pan. Add the onion and sausage and cook over
a low heat, stirring occasionally, for 5 minutes, until the onion has
softened. Add the garlic, tomatoes and oregano and cook for a further
5 minutes.

2 Pour in the stock or water, season to taste with salt, and cook, stirring
frequently, until completely heated through.

3 Add the bread and coriander and cook, stirring, until the bread is fully
incorporated. Serve immediately.

COOK'S TIPS

• To peel a tomato, cut a cross in the top, immerse in boiling water for
1 minute and refresh in iced water. Then peel off the skin.

• You can add a poached egg to each bowl just before serving.

Seafood Soup Sopa do mar

1 Heat 30ml/2 tbsp of the olive oil in a large pan. Add the prawn heads and fish bones and cook over a low heat, stirring frequently, for 5 minutes.

2 Add the mixed vegetables, bay leaf and peppercorns and cook for a further 5 minutes, mashing the prawn heads with a wooden spoon.

3 Pour in the wine and 2 litres/3½ pints/8¾ cups water. Bring to the boil, then lower the heat and simmer gently for 1 hour.

4 Add the fish bones and gradually bring back to the boil. Lower the heat and simmer very gently for 20 minutes. Remove the pan from the heat and strain the stock into a bowl.

5 Heat the remaining olive oil in a large, clean pan. Add the green and red peppers, onion and tomatoes, and cook over a low heat, stirring occasionally, for 5 minutes, until softened. Add the garlic and thyme, pour in the stock and bring just to the boil.

6 Add the clams and squid and cook for 2–3 minutes, until the clams have opened. Add the fish and prawns and cook for 5 minutes more, until the fish is opaque. Sprinkle with the coriander and serve immediately.

Serves 6

60ml/4 tbsp olive oil
2kg/4½lb prawn (shrimp) heads and
    fish bones
1kg/2¼lb mixed onions, carrots,
    leek, and garlic, coarsely chopped
1 bay leaf
6 black peppercorns
105ml/7 tbsp dry white wine
1 green and 1 red (bell) pepper,
    seeded and finely diced
1 onion, chopped
2 ripe tomatoes, peeled and diced
1 garlic clove, chopped
15ml/1 tbsp chopped fresh thyme
185g/6½oz live clams, scrubbed
125g/4¼oz prepared squid
300g/11oz white fish fillet, cut into
    chunks
12 prawns (shrimp), peeled
chopped fresh coriander (cilantro),
    to garnish

Rich seafood soups are prepared in a variety of ways all along the coast of Portugal. Whenever you prepare a dish with prawns or fillet fish, save the heads and bones and freeze them until you have enough to make a flavoursome stock, such as the one used in this recipe. Some versions of this seafood soup add diced potato to the stock, while others add rice or noodles.

Hare Soup Sopa de Lebre

1 Cut the hare or rabbit into pieces. Wash well and pat dry with kitchen paper. Slice one carrot and dice the other. Heat 45ml/3 tbsp of the olive oil in a large pan. Add the pieces of hare and cook, turning occasionally, for about 10 minutes, until golden brown all over.

2 Drain off the oil from the pan. Add the port, onion, leek, sliced carrot, garlic, peppercorns and bay leaf, and pour in enough water to cover. Bring to the boil, then lower the heat and simmer gently for 1½ hours.

Serves 6

1 hare or rabbit
2 carrots
75ml/5 tbsp olive oil
75ml/5 tbsp dry white port
1 onion, sliced
1 leek, sliced
1 garlic clove, chopped
6 black peppercorns
1 bay leaf
15ml/1 tbsp cornflour (cornstarch)
1 turnip, diced
3 heads pak choi (bok choy), cut into strips
200g/7oz oyster mushrooms, sliced
300g/11oz/2¼ cups cooked haricot beans
1 small bunch of fresh peppermint, chopped
salt

3 Strain the stock into a bowl and reserve the meat. Remove the bones from the meat and cut the meat into small pieces. Return the stock to the rinsed-out pan and set over a low heat.

4 Mix the cornflour to a paste with 30ml/2 tbsp water. Stir it into the stock and season to taste with salt.

5 Cook the remaining carrot, the turnip and pak choi in separate pans of boiling water until just tender, then add to the stock.

6 Meanwhile, heat the remaining oil in another pan, add the mushrooms and cook over a low heat, stirring occasionally, for 5–7 minutes. Add them to the stock with the beans. Stir in the reserved meat and the peppermint, heat through gently and serve.

COOK'S TIP

For ease of cooking, ask your butcher to portion your hare or rabbit.

This rich soup is a great favourite in the centre and south of Portugal. Served with fresh bread, it is a meal in itself. The soup can be made with other game, such as pheasant, and the white beans can be replaced with lentils, which combine excellently with game. If available, use wild peppermint for its pronounced aroma and flavour.

Salt Cod with Potato Mash Gratin
Bacalhau à Conde da Guarda

Serves 8

1kg/2¼lb potatoes, unpeeled
800g/1¾lb salt cod, soaked
105ml/7 tbsp olive oil
200ml/7fl oz/scant 1 cup single
   (light) cream
2 garlic cloves, chopped
1 small bunch of parsley, chopped
pinch of freshly grated nutmeg
salt

This recipe is reminiscent of the well-known French salt cod purée, brandade. *Many similar dishes are produced in other Mediterranean countries, using salt or dried cod, which is also known as stockfish. Serve with an assortment of lettuce, seasoned with parsley vinaigrette. A smaller portion of this recipe is ideal as an appetizer.*

1 Cook the potatoes in a large pan of lightly salted boiling water for 20–30 minutes, until tender. Drain well, then peel and mash with a fork. Meanwhile, preheat the oven to 200°C/400°F/Gas 6.

2 Bring another large pan of water to the boil. Add the fish and bring back to the boil, then immediately remove the pan from the heat. Leave to stand for 5 minutes.

3 Remove the fish from the pan with a slotted spatula and leave to cool slightly. Remove and discard the skin and bones.

4 Mix the fish with the potatoes, then blend in the olive oil and cream and the garlic. Stir in the parsley and nutmeg and season with salt, if necessary. Spoon the mixture into an ovenproof dish and bake for about 20 minutes. Serve hot.

Salt Cod with a Cornbread Crust
Bacalhau com broa

Serves 4

150ml/¼ pint/⅔ cup olive oil, plus
    extra for brushing
300g/11oz/6 cups cornbread crumbs
30ml/2 tbsp chopped fresh parsley
1 garlic clove, finely chopped
15ml/1 tbsp sweet paprika
4 pieces of salt cod cut from the
    centre, about 200g/7oz each
cooked cabbage and baked potatoes,
    to serve

*The centre part of salt cod,
preferably from an adult fish,
provides the plump fillet that
is most prized in Portugal.
The classic way to serve it is
chargrilled and then drizzled
with plenty of olive oil.
Another option is to add
seafood, such as shrimp
and clams. In this recipe, the
cornbread crust protects
the cod from drying out,
retaining all its juices.*

1 Preheat the oven to 200°C/400°F/Gas 6. Brush a shallow ovenproof dish with oil.

2 Mix together the breadcrumbs, parsley, garlic, paprika and olive oil to a thick paste in a bowl. (You may not need all the oil.)

3 Spread this paste all over the fish, place in the prepared dish and bake for about 20 minutes. Serve with cabbage and baked potatoes.

Braised Octopus with Rice
Polvo assado com arroz no forno

Serves 4

1 octopus, about 1.6kg/3½lb
150ml/¼ pint/⅔ cup olive oil
2 onions, chopped
300g/11oz/generous 1½ cups long
    grain rice
1 bay leaf

For the stock

2 onions, quartered
1 leek, chopped
3 garlic cloves, crushed
10 black peppercorns
2 bay leaves
pinch of salt

1 Rinse the octopus in plenty of water and cut off the body. Turn the body inside out and pull out and discard the entrails. Remove the little strips from the sides of the body. Rinse thoroughly again and turn the right way out. Squeeze out the beak. Beat the tentacles lightly with a rolling pin or the flat side of a meat mallet.

2 Half fill a pan with water and add all the ingredients for the stock. Bring to the boil, then lower the heat and simmer for 10 minutes.

3 Add the octopus and bring back to the boil. Lower the heat slightly so that the liquid continues to boil and cook for 1 hour. Check with a fork to see if the octopus is tender. If not, cook for a little longer but check frequently because it will toughen if overcooked.

4 Strain the stock into a bowl and reserve. Discard the flavourings. Chop the octopus body and cut the tentacles into short lengths, keeping the two parts separate. Preheat the oven to 160°C/325°F/Gas 3.

5 Heat 50ml/2fl oz/¼ cup of the olive oil in a flameproof casserole. Add the onions and cook over a low heat, stirring occasionally, for 10 minutes, until lightly browned. Add the rice, the octopus body, the bay leaf and 600ml/1 pint/2½ cups of the reserved stock. Transfer the casserole to the oven and braise for 30 minutes.

6 Meanwhile, place the tentacles in an ovenproof dish, pour the remaining olive oil over them and heat through in the oven. Combine with the rice mixture before serving.

While it has a delicate flavour, octopus also has a reputation for being chewy. This texture depends on its quality and how it is cooked.

Stuffed Squid Lulas recheadas

1 Rinse the squid under cold running water, then pull the head away from the body – the entrails will come away with the head. Cut off the tentacles and squeeze out the beak. Chop the tentacles and discard the beak. Pull out and discard the transparent quill from the body sac and clean out any remaining membrane. Rinse the body sac and peel off the skin.

2 Heat 50ml/2fl oz/¼ cup of the olive oil in a pan. Add half the onions and half the garlic and cook over a low heat, stirring occasionally, for 5 minutes, until softened. Add the chopped tentacles, ham and sausage or bacon and cook for a few minutes more. Stir in a quarter of the tomatoes and all the rice. Mix well and remove the pan from the heat.

3 Spoon the filling into the body sacs of the squid, filling them just over half full. Secure the openings with wooden cocktail sticks (toothpicks).

4 Heat the remaining oil in a large pan. Add the remaining onions and garlic and cook over a low heat, stirring occasionally, for 5 minutes, until softened. Add the bay leaf and remaining tomatoes and pour in about 150ml/¼ pint/⅔ cup water to top up. Stir in the parsley and add the stuffed squid. Season with salt and simmer gently for about 20 minutes, until tender. Serve with cooked potatoes.

VARIATION
As an alternative to stewing the squid, try them grilled (broiled) with a little olive oil and sprinkled with the chopped parsley.

Characteristic to most of the Portuguese coast, the preparation of this recipe can vary considerably. The squid meat can be replaced by squid tentacles. The stuffing can also be prepared with other fish, such as hake, as long as you leave out the tomato in the stuffing.

Serves 4

1kg/2¼lb squid, preferably about 10cm/4in long
150ml/¼ pint/⅔ cup olive oil
4 onions, chopped
2 garlic cloves, chopped
100g/3¾oz cured ham, chopped
150g/5oz sausage or bacon, chopped
4 large ripe tomatoes, peeled and chopped
100g/3¾oz/generous ½ cup cooked rice
1 bay leaf
1 bunch of parsley, chopped
salt
cooked potatoes, to serve

Juicy Seafood Rice
Arroz de marisco

1 Heat the olive oil in a large pan. Add the onion and green pepper and cook over a low heat, stirring occasionally, for 5 minutes, until softened. Add the tomato and the stock and bring to the boil.

2 Open the clams, cockles and mussels. The easiest way do this is by steaming them briefly in a little water and removing them from their shells as soon as they open. It's best to do this in small batches. Discard any shells that do not open. Reserve the shellfish meat, keeping the shells to one side.

3 Add the rice to the pan, bring back to the boil and cook for about 12 minutes, until tender. The mixture should be moist; if necessary, add more stock. Add all the seafood and the coriander, heat through briefly and serve, decorated with the seafood shells, if you like.

Serves 4

50ml/2fl oz/¼ cup olive oil

1 onion, chopped

1 green (bell) pepper, seeded and chopped

1 tomato, peeled and chopped

1 litre/1¾ pints/4 cups shellfish stock

200g/7oz live clams, scrubbed

200g/7oz live cockles, scrubbed

200g/7oz live mussels, scrubbed and beards removed

300g/11oz/generous 1½ cups risotto rice

400g/14oz cooked peeled prawns (shrimp)

30ml/2 tbsp chopped fresh coriander (cilantro)

All along the Portuguese coastline, any restaurant will serve this rice dish, made with the best produce the sea can supply. It is often served in the pan in which it is cooked, or in a terracotta pot placed in the centre of the table and shared by everyone. The rice used is carolino rice, which is similar to Italian risotto rice, but long grain rice is also good.

Roast Pork Ribs with *Milhos*
Entrecosto assado com milhos

Serves 4

1kg/2¼lb pork ribs, cut into
  2cm/¾in slices
2 bay leaves
3 garlic cloves, chopped
1 litre/1¾ pints/4 cups olive oil
sea salt

For the *milhos*

50ml/2fl oz/¼ cup olive oil
1 onion, finely chopped
2 ripe tomatoes, peeled and cut into
  quarters
750ml/1¼ pints/3 cups chicken
  stock or water
250g/9oz/2¼ cups coarse cornmeal

1 Preheat the oven to 140°C/275°F/Gas 1. Place the meat on a baking tray or in a shallow ovenproof dish about 5cm/2in deep. Add the bay leaves, season with salt, and sprinkle with the garlic. Pour over the olive oil and roast for about 2 hours.

2 Towards the end of the roasting time, prepare the *milhos*. Heat the oil in a large pan. Add the onion and cook over a low heat, stirring occasionally, for 5–10 minutes, until the onion is soft and translucent. Add the tomatoes and cook for a few more minutes.

3 Add 500ml/17fl oz/generous 2 cups of the stock or water and bring to the boil. Sprinkle in the cornmeal, whisking constantly. As the mixture starts to thicken, add the remaining stock. Season to taste with salt, but if you are using stock rather than water, you will probably not need any. Simmer for about 3 minutes, until creamy.

4 Remove the meat from the oven, place on a dish and serve immediately, handing round the *milhos* separately at the table.

COOK'S TIP
Serve the *milhos* as soon as it becomes creamy, as otherwise it tends to thicken.

It may sound inappropriate to cook fatty meat in a lot of olive oil, but this produces excellent results, because the meat becomes smooth and the fat reduces. Milhos, the Portuguese equivalent of polenta, is prepared all over the country. If coarse cornmeal is used, the results are usually a little more liquid than with fine cornmeal.

Pork Confit with Asparagus Bread Mash
Carne de porco no pingue com migas de espargos

1 Place the pork in a bowl. Mix together the paprika paste, wine, garlic and bay leaves, add to the pork and leave to marinate for 6 hours.

2 Melt the fat in a deep saucepan. Add the meat, cover the saucepan and cook over a low heat for 2 hours.

3 Meanwhile, prepare the mash. Cut off the crust from the bread and cut the bread into cubes.

4 Transfer 30ml/2 tbsp of the fat from the meat to a frying pan and heat. Add the bacon and garlic and cook, stirring occasionally, for about 5 minutes, until the bacon is lightly browned. Add the bread and 400ml/14floz/1⅔ cups water and blend well with a wooden spoon. You may have to add a little more water or fat to get a smooth texture like potato mash.

5 Add the asparagus and the coriander, and roll the mixture so that it forms the shape of an omelette.

6 Remove the meat with a slotted spoon and serve with the mash.

COOK'S TIP
Pork cooked this way, once it is completely covered with the fat, can be kept for several weeks is the refrigerator.

This is a speciality from Alentejo, in the south of Portugal. The asparagus bread mash can also be made with other ingredients, such as tomatoes or wild herbs. Whatever ingredients are used, it is only when the mash achieves the shape of an omelette that it is ready.

Serves 4

700g/1lb 9oz pork shoulder, cut into 40g/1½oz cubes
60ml/4 tbsp paprika paste
50ml/2fl oz/¼ cup white wine
2 garlic cloves, chopped
2 bay leaves
1kg/2¼lb pork or duck fat
sea salt

For the green asparagus bread mash

800g/1¾lb day-old white bread
100g/3¾oz/generous ½ cup diced bacon
1 garlic clove, chopped
400g/14oz green asparagus, cooked
15ml/1 tbsp chopped fresh coriander (cilantro)

Lamb Shank with Chickpeas, Vegetables and Sausages Pernil de Borrego com cozido de grão

Serves 4

50ml/2fl oz/¼ cup olive oil
4 lamb shanks, about 275g/10oz each
4 onions, thinly sliced
2 garlic cloves, chopped
50ml/2fl oz/¼ cup white wine
1 bay leaf
1 *chouriço* sausage
125g/4¼oz bacon, cut into four pieces
2 carrots, sliced
125g/4¼oz green beans, cut into short lengths
2 turnips, diced
400g/14oz/2⅓ cups cooked chickpeas
salt
1 small bunch of mint, chopped, to garnish

1 Heat half the olive oil in a pan big enough to hold the lamb shanks. Add the lamb shanks and gently cook over a medium heat, turning occasionally, for 5–8 minutes, until lightly coloured. Remove them from the pan and reserve.

2 Discard the oil and wipe out the pan with kitchen paper. Place the remaining olive oil, the onions and garlic in the pan and return the lamb shanks. Add the white wine, bay leaf, sausage and bacon, then cover and cook over a low heat, stirring occasionally, for about 2 hours, until tender. Season with salt to taste.

3 Cook the carrots, green beans and turnips in salted boiling water until tender. Drain.

4 Remove the sausage from the pan and cut into 2cm/¾in slices. Return the sausage to the pan, add the vegetables and chickpeas, and cook for a further 5 minutes so that all the flavours blend. Transfer to a warm serving dish and garnish with the mint.

Lamb stews are widespread in central and southern Portugal. They differ slightly in the choice of spices, but the trick is to keep them simple. Slow cooking times are one of the secrets and it is also important to use a lot of thinly sliced onions, as well as black pepper, paprika, bay leaves and garlic to add flavour. After cooking, the onions will have become a juicy sauce.

Rib-Eye Steak with Ham, Garlic and Bay Leaves Bife do acém à Portuguesa

Serves 4

50ml/2fl oz/¼ cup olive oil

4 rib-eye steaks, each weighing about 240g/8½oz

4 garlic cloves, lightly crushed

4 small bay leaves

120ml/4fl oz/½ cup white wine

8 slices of cured ham

sea salt

deep-fried potato slices or baked potatoes, to serve

This is a classic steak recipe, traditionally prepared in a terracotta dish. If you have some beef stock available, add it to the sauce to make it richer. Rib-eye is a fantastic cut as its fat melts during cooking, flavouring the meat. Salt the meat immediately before frying, using sea salt instead of the refined variety, as it improves the taste.

1 Heat half the oil in a large pan. Lightly season the steaks with sea salt, add them to the pan and cook until done to your liking (use about 3 minutes each side for rare and 4 minutes each side for medium). Remove the steaks from the pan and keep them warm.

2 Add the remaining oil, the garlic and bay leaves, then pour in the wine and cook for a few minutes more.

3 Place the steaks on warm plates, top each with two slices of ham and spoon the sauce over them. Serve immediately, with the potatoes of your choice.

Chicken Thighs with Cabbage and Chickpeas
Coxa de frango com penca e grão

Serves 4

105ml/7 tbsp olive oil
1 onion, chopped
100g/3¾oz/generous ½ cup diced
    bacon
1 sausage, diced
3 carrots, diced
2 garlic cloves, chopped
2 bay leaves
2 thyme sprigs
8 black peppercorns
8 chicken thighs or 4 chicken legs
1 cabbage
250g/9oz/1½ cups cooked
    chickpeas
sea salt

This meal is cooked in one pot and is ideal for serving to large numbers of people. The combination of meat with chickpeas and cabbage provides a nourishing dish. Sometimes pasta is added.

1 Heat the olive oil in a large pan. Add the onion and gently cook, stirring occasionally, for 5 minutes, until softened. Increase the heat to medium, add the bacon, sausage, carrots, garlic, bay leaves, thyme sprigs and peppercorns and cook, stirring constantly, for a few minutes more.

2 Add the chicken, pour in enough water just to cover and season with salt. Bring just to the boil, then lower the heat, cover and simmer gently for 40 minutes. Remove the chicken and keep warm. Reserve the cooking liquid but remove and discard the bay leaves and thyme sprigs.

3 Meanwhile, prepare the cabbage. Cut in half and cut out the central hard part, then separate the leaves and cut into large slices. Cook in lightly salted boiling water for about 10 minutes. Drain well.

4 Mix the cabbage with the chickpeas, then add the reserved cooking liquid. Heat through, then serve the chicken with the vegetables.

Partridge in Marinade 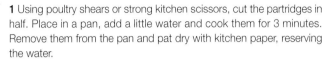 Perdiz de escabeche

Serves 4

4 partridges
105ml/7 tbsp olive oil
2 onions, thinly sliced
2 garlic cloves, chopped
1 carrot, scraped and sliced
    lengthways
2 bay leaves
8–12 grains of black pepper
4 cloves
105ml/7 tbsp white wine vinegar
50ml/2fl oz/¼ cup white wine
1 small bunch of parsley, chopped
sea salt

1 Using poultry shears or strong kitchen scissors, cut the partridges in half. Place in a pan, add a little water and cook them for 3 minutes. Remove them from the pan and pat dry with kitchen paper, reserving the water.

2 Heat half the olive oil in a frying pan. Add the partridges and cook, turning occasionally, for about 10 minutes, until golden brown.

3 Meanwhile, heat the remaining oil in a large pan. Add the onions, garlic, carrot, bay leaves, black pepper and cloves and cook over a low heat, stirring occasionally, for 5 minutes.

4 Add the vinegar, wine and partridges to the pan. Add enough of the reserved cooking water to cover and then bring to the boil. Lower the heat, cover the pan and simmer for about 10 minutes. Season with salt and sprinkle with parsley. Remove from the heat and either serve straight away or leave to cool, transfer to a covered dish and store in the refrigerator for up to 2–3 days before eating cold.

VARIATION
The onion base is integral to this recipe, but can be adapted using tomatoes, carrots, wild mushrooms, aubergine (eggplant) or bacon.

Partridge is the favourite game bird of Portugal and it is commonly available throughout the country. It is usually cooked in a stew and each game hunter claims to have his own secret recipe. In the Douro region, which is the home of port wine, they like to marinate the bird in an intense ruby port before cooking. This recipe subtly enhances the natural flavour of the game. The dish can be served cold with a salad and bread, or alternatively served warm with potatoes.

Sweet Rice Arroz Doce

Serves 8

250g/9oz/1¼ cups short-grain rice
thinly pared rind of 1 lemon
1 cinnamon stick
pinch of salt
1.2 litres/2 pints/5 cups milk
150g/5oz/⅔ cup sugar
4 egg yolks
ground cinnamon, for sprinkling

1 Put the rice, lemon rind, cinnamon stick and salt in a pan and pour in 500ml/17fl oz/ generous 2 cups water. Bring to the boil and simmer until almost dry.

2 Add 1 litre/1¾ pints/4 cups of the milk and the sugar to the pan with the rice and continue to cook, stirring frequently.

3 Meanwhile, mix the egg yolks with the remaining milk in a jug or pitcher. When the rice is beginning to become dry, stir in the egg yolk mixture.

4 Remove the pan from the heat, pour the rice mixture into a tray and leave to cool and set.

5 Cut into squares and sprinkle with cinnamon. Serve in a deep plate.

This traditional dessert is a Christmas speciality that can also be prepared throughout the year. Pre-cooking the rice in water allows it to better absorb the milk and sugar during the cooking process. The rice is a similar shape to risotto rice, with a high amount of starch. The dish can also be made with a type of hair-thin pasta called aletria, often used in Portuguese cooking.

Honey Pudding with Ricotta Pudim de mel com requeijão batido

1 Preheat the oven to 180°C/350°F/Gas 4. Brush eight 40cm/1½in square moulds with olive oil and sprinkle with breadcrumbs, shaking out the excess.

2 Beat the eggs in a bowl, then beat in all the remaining ingredients until well blended.

3 Divide the mixture among the prepared moulds and place them in a roasting pan. Add sufficient boiling water to come about halfway up the sides of the moulds and bake for about 15 minutes, until risen.

4 Give the puddings approximately 5 minutes to fully stabilise and then turn them out while they are still warm. Sprinkle with icing sugar and serve with ricotta cheese or other fresh cheese.

Serves 8
olive oil, for brushing
breadcrumbs, for sprinkling
8 eggs
300g/11oz/1½ cups sugar
50g/2oz/2½ tbsp molasses
50g/2oz/¼ cup clear honey
2.5ml/½ tsp ground cinnamon
5ml/1 tsp dried yeast
icing (confectioners') sugar, to serve
ricotta or other fresh cheese, to serve

This recipe originated on the islands of Madeira and Azores, where similar versions are made. The flavour of this pudding is characterized by molasses. It is particularly delicious served with requeijão, a fresh cheese similar to ricotta, which provides an appealing contrast. It is also excellent accompanied by pumpkin marmalade.

Sponge Cake Pão de ló

Serves 6
melted butter, for brushing
125g/4¼oz/generous 1 cup plain
 (all-purpose) flour
6 eggs
12 egg yolks
240g/8½oz/generous 2 cups icing
 (confectioner's) sugar

For the cinnamon sauce
105ml/7 tbsp milk
45ml/3 tbsp icing (confectioner's)
 sugar
2 egg yolks
pinch of ground cinnamon

1 Preheat the oven to 160°C/325°F/Gas 3. Brush a round cake tin or pan, 20cm/8in in diameter and 5cm/2in deep, with melted butter. Line with baking parchment and brush with melted butter again.

2 Sift the flour into a bowl and set aside. Beat the eggs and yolks with the sugar in another bowl until light and fluffy. Gradually fold in the flour.

3 Spoon the mixture into the prepared tin and bake for 25 minutes. Leave to cool completely in the tin.

4 Meanwhile, make the cinnamon sauce. Put all the ingredients in a heatproof bowl. Set the bowl over a pan of barely simmering water and beat well until slightly thickened. Taste and beat in more cinnamon if required. Leave to cool.

5 To serve, remove the cake from the tin, using the baking parchment to ease it out. Cut into slices, bearing in mind that the centre is moist, and place on individual plates. Serve with the cinnamon sauce.

VARIATION
Melt 125g/4¼oz of bitter chocolate and 125g/4¼oz of butter in a bain-marie, and fold into the cake mixture at the end of step 2. Cook as before and freeze lightly (for about 15 minutes) before serving to produce a delightful chocolate sponge.

There are many ways of preparing sponge cake and lots of villages have their own recipe, usually bearing the village's name. The differences are in the proportion of sugar, eggs and flour and – critically – the cooking time. This is a version from Ovar, located below Porto on the coast, which is also well known for its carnival. A very popular dish, it is distinctive for leaving the cake moist in the centre.

Angels' Cheeks with Oranges
Papos de anjo com laranja em calda

Serves 6
3 oranges
200g/7oz/1 cup sugar
melted butter, for brushing
5 egg yolks
1 egg
24 raspberries, to serve

1 Wash the oranges thoroughly, then remove the rind with a citrus zester.

2 Put the orange rind and sugar in a pan and add 200ml/7fl oz/scant 1 cup water. Bring to the boil, stirring until the sugar has dissolved, then boil, without stirring for 5 minutes. Remove the pan from the heat.

3 Remove all the pith from the oranges and cut out the segments. Place in a heatproof bowl and add the syrup.

4 Preheat the oven to 160°C/325°F/Gas 3. Brush six ramekins, traditionally half-spheres measuring 70 x 35mm/3 x 1½in, with melted butter.

5 Beat the egg yolks and egg for about 10 minutes. Divide among the prepared ramekins, place in a tray with about 1cm/½in of warm water and bake for about 15 minutes, until golden.

6 To serve, divide the oranges in syrup among individual plates, turn out an "angel's cheek" on top of each serving, and add a few raspberries.

This easy-to-prepare dessert is delightful served with oranges and raspberries, but will also go well with other fruits. As the "cheeks" are made without sugar, the sweetness comes from the fruit you serve them with. Many Portuguese desserts originated in convents, which explains the origin of the frequent religious references in the recipe names.

Dreams Sonhos

1 Heat the milk until just lukewarm. Cream the yeast with the tepid milk and set aside.

2 Sift the flour into a bowl and make a well in the centre. Add the eggs and gradually incorporate the flour, then add the milk mixture, brandy and pumpkin stock and mix well. The mixture should drop thickly from a spoon. Leave to rest for 30 minutes.

3 Heat the oil for deep-frying to 180–190°C/350–375°F or until a cube of day-old bread browns in 40 seconds. Stir the mixture again and, using two spoons, shape small pieces into little balls and place in the hot oil until browned.

4 Remove with a slotted spoon, drain well, sprinkle with sugar and cinnamon and serve.

Serves 8–10
750ml/1¼ pints/3 cups milk
20g/¾oz fresh yeast
750g/1lb 10oz/6½ cups plain
   (all-purpose) flour
8 eggs, lightly beaten
50ml/2fl oz/¼ cup brandy
750ml/1¼ pints/3 cups pumpkin
   stock
vegetable oil, for deep-frying
sugar and ground cinnamon, for
   sprinkling

The pumpkin stock gives a unique taste to these fried balls.
They taste wonderful with a little sugar, especially when they
are still warm from the oven. Dreams are traditionally made
on Christmas Eve before the family gathers for the evening
meal. A glass of tawny port is an excellent complement
to this sweet dessert.

Almond Biscuits Arrepiados

Makes 25

500g/1¼lb/5 cups ground almonds
250g/9oz/generous 1 cup light
    brown sugar
5ml/1 tsp ground cinnamon
2–3 eggs, lightly beaten
grated rind of 1 lemon

*These almond biscuits or
cookies perfectly
complement both coffee
and an after-supper glass of
port. If you prefer them
flatter, add some butter so
that they drain while baking.
Using roughly ground
almonds gives them a
crispier texture. Alternatively,
make them with a mixture of
hazelnuts and almonds, or
just hazelnuts.*

1 Preheat the oven to 180°C/350°F/Gas 4. Mix all the ingredients together until blended, using enough beaten egg to make a stiff paste. Shape into little balls.

2 Place the balls on a non-stick baking sheet, spaced well apart, and gently flatten them. Bake for about 10 minutes, until light brown. Leave to stand for 2 minutes, then transfer to a wire rack to cool completely.

Nutritional notes

Tomato Salad with Marinated Peppers and Oregano: Energy 119kcal/494kJ; Protein 1.4g; Carbohydrate 6.9g, of which sugars 6.7g; Fat 9.7g, of which saturates 1.5g; Cholesterol 0mg; Calcium 17mg; Fibre 2.1g; Sodium 12mg.

Marinated Mushrooms: Energy 130kcal/541kJ; Protein 12.1g; Carbohydrate 3.1g, of which sugars 1g; Fat 7.8g, of which saturates 1.5g; Cholesterol 29mg; Calcium 20mg; Fibre 1.8g; Sodium 607mg.

Green Beans Tempura: Energy 227kcal/945kJ; Protein 5.8g; Carbohydrate 22.6g, of which sugars 2.7g; Fat 13.2g, of which saturates 1.8g; Cholesterol 48mg; Calcium 78mg; Fibre 3g; Sodium 18mg.

Sardines in Onion and Tomato Marinade: Energy 335kcal/1392kJ; Protein 21.2g; Carbohydrate 4.3g, of which sugars 1.1g; Fat 26g, of which saturates 5.1g; Cholesterol 0mg; Calcium 92mg; Fibre 0.5g; Sodium 123mg.

Clams with Fresh Coriander: Energy 197kcal/816kJ; Protein 8.9g; Carbohydrate 2.3g, of which sugars 0.4g; Fat 17g, of which saturates 2.5g; Cholesterol 34mg; Calcium 63mg; Fibre 0.9g; Sodium 605mg.

Small Chicken Pies: Energy 368kcal/1534kJ; Protein 24.5g; Carbohydrate 18.3g, of which sugars 1.2g; Fat 22.8g, of which saturates 4.3g; Cholesterol 109mg; Calcium 44mg; Fibre 0.2g; Sodium 547mg.

Chestnut and White Bean Soup: Energy 184kcal/773kJ; Protein 6.2g; Carbohydrate 20.5g, of which sugars 3.1g; Fat 9.2g, of which saturates 1.4g; Cholesterol 0mg; Calcium 39mg; Fibre 5.1g; Sodium 8mg.

Green Bean and Cabbage Soup: Energy 239kcal/998kJ; Protein 6.2g; Carbohydrate 34.2g, of which sugars 11.7g; Fat 9.6g, of which saturates 1.4g; Cholesterol 0mg; Calcium 96mg; Fibre 6.1g; Sodium 20mg.

Tomato Soup: Energy 233kcal/971kJ; Protein 5.4g; Carbohydrate 19.1g, of which sugars 4.9g; Fat 15.5g, of which saturates 3.6g; Cholesterol 9mg; Calcium 50mg; Fibre 1.7g; Sodium 695mg.

Seafood Soup: Energy 267kcal/1112kJ; Protein 20.1g; Carbohydrate 25.2g, of which sugars 18.7g; Fat 9g, of which saturates 1.3g; Cholesterol 96mg; Calcium 96mg; Fibre 4.8g; Sodium 262mg.

Hare Soup: Energy 297kcal/1242kJ; Protein 24g; Carbohydrate 18.7g, of which sugars 8.5g; Fat 12.9g, of which saturates 2.9g; Cholesterol 69mg; Calcium 159mg; Fibre 6.4g; Sodium 299mg.

Salt Cod with Potato Mash Gratin: Energy 366kcal/1535kJ; Protein 35.9g; Carbohydrate 21.4g, of which sugars 2.4g; Fat 15.8g, of which saturates 4.7g; Cholesterol 73mg; Calcium 65mg; Fibre 1.7g; Sodium 423mg.

Salt Cod with a Corn Bread Crust: Energy 781kcal/3290kJ; Protein 74.6g; Carbohydrate 59.8g, of which sugars 2.2g; Fat 28.9g, of which saturates 4.1g; Cholesterol 118mg; Calcium 173mg; Fibre 2.3g; Sodium 1376mg.

Braised Octopus with Rice: Energy 871kcal/3646kJ; Protein 78.8g; Carbohydrate 69.7g, of which sugars 7g; Fat 30.9g, of which saturates 4.8g; Cholesterol 192mg; Calcium 178mg; Fibre 1.8g; Sodium 95mg.

Stuffed Squid: Energy 715kcal/2987kJ; Protein 50.8g; Carbohydrate 33.5g, of which sugars 15.1g; Fat 43.1g, of which saturates 9.6g; Cholesterol 595mg; Calcium 111mg; Fibre 4g; Sodium 875mg.

Juicy Seafood Rice: Energy 484kcal/2027kJ; Protein 32g; Carbohydrate 64.6g, of which sugars 4.2g; Fat 10.5g, of which saturates 1.5g; Cholesterol 213mg; Calcium 215mg; Fibre 1.7g; Sodium 292mg.

Roast Pork Ribs with *Milhos*: Energy 1035kcal/4304kJ; Protein 53.2g; Carbohydrate 48.4g, of which sugars 2.4g; Fat 69.5g, of which saturates 17.9g; Cholesterol 165mg; Calcium 47mg; Fibre 2.1g; Sodium 250mg.

Pork Confit with Green Asparagus Bread Mash: Energy 925kcal/3899kJ; Protein 63.5g; Carbohydrate 105.9g, of which sugars 7.2g; Fat 29.9g, of which saturates 9.4g; Cholesterol 135mg; Calcium 289mg; Fibre 4.7g; Sodium 1554mg.

Lamb Shank with Chickpeas, Vegetables and Sausages: Energy 688kcal/2868kJ; Protein 39.3g; Carbohydrate 34.9g, of which sugars 11.8g; Fat 43.7g, of which saturates 14.6g; Cholesterol 115mg; Calcium 134mg; Fibre 7.9g; Sodium 1143mg.

Rib-Eye Steak with Ham, Garlic and Bay Leaves: Energy 539kcal/2246kJ; Protein 57.7g; Carbohydrate 4.5g, of which sugars 0.8g; Fat 30.2g, of which saturates 10g; Cholesterol 145mg; Calcium 21mg; Fibre 1g; Sodium 446mg.

Chicken Thighs with Cabbage and Chickpeas: Energy 456kcal/1894kJ; Protein 19.6g; Carbohydrate 23.6g, of which sugars 10.5g; Fat 32g, of which saturates 7g; Cholesterol 55mg; Calcium 126mg; Fibre 6.4g; Sodium 643mg.

Partridge in Marinade: Energy 938kcal/3919kJ; Protein 123.1g; Carbohydrate 12.3g, of which sugars 9.2g; Fat 43.4g, of which saturates 8.8g; Cholesterol 0mg; Calcium 218mg; Fibre 3g; Sodium 345mg.

Sweet Rice: Energy 286kcal/1203kJ; Protein 9g; Carbohydrate 51.6g, of which sugars 26.7g; Fat 5.5g, of which saturates 2.4g; Cholesterol 110mg; Calcium 208mg; Fibre 0g; Sodium 70mg.

Honey Pudding with Ricotta: Energy 267kcal/1133kJ; Protein 7g; Carbohydrate 50.7g, of which sugars 48.2g; Fat 5.7g, of which saturates 1.6g; Cholesterol 190mg; Calcium 88mg; Fibre 0.1g; Sodium 108mg.

Sponge Cake: Energy 485kcal/2041kJ; Protein 15.8g; Carbohydrate 67.4g, of which sugars 51.5g; Fat 18.9g, of which saturates 5.4g; Cholesterol 662mg; Calcium 159mg; Fibre 0.7g; Sodium 102mg.

Angels' Cheeks with Oranges: Energy 217kcal/917kJ; Protein 4.3g; Carbohydrate 39.9g, of which sugars 39.9g; Fat 5.6g, of which saturates 1.6g; Cholesterol 200mg; Calcium 70mg; Fibre 1g; Sodium 24mg.

Dreams: Energy 439kcal/1850kJ; Protein 14.6g; Carbohydrate 61.8g, of which sugars 4.7g; Fat 15.5g, of which saturates 3.2g; Cholesterol 157mg; Calcium 218mg; Fibre 2.3g; Sodium 91mg.

Almond Biscuits: Energy 168.4kcal/702.4kJ; Protein 4.8; Carbohydrate 11.9g, of which sugars 11.3g; Fat 11.6g, of which saturates 1g; Cholesterol 15.2mg; Calcium 56mg; Fibre 1.5g; Sodium 9.1mg.

Index